Thug Kitchen

Eat Like you give a F*CK

AMARPREET SINGH

THE THOUGHT FLAME
TURNING SPARK INTO FLAME

info@thethoughtflame.com

www.thethoughtflame.com

Table of Contents

Introduction

There are those out there that claim that being Vegan is a lifestyle choice, and the truth of the matter is that this is the truth. If you are reading this book then you are either a vegan or want to become a vegan in the near future.

The importance of being fit and healthy is now being brought into the spotlight since the cases of obesity and food related illness have been on the rise at the start of the past decade. Instead of treating obesity or an unhealthy lifestyle that is something that is just bothersome, it should be treated more as an epidemic as it affect millions of people world wide. Many of these "victims" range in age from elderly to toddlers.

Instead of focusing on all of the negative aspects of unhealthy eating, this book is aimed at highlighting the positive aspects of healthy eating. We will look in depth on how to feed your body with the food it deserves considering our bodies are more our friends than anything. As our friend we only want the best for our bodies and do not to force food into it that is only going to harm it in the long run.

This book focuses on the positive aspects of living a vegan lifestyle and how it can help you to not only become healthier, but how it can help you to lose weight in the process.

So, what are you waiting for? Let's get started!

Chapter One: What The F**K Does It Mean To Be Vegan?

Have you ever looked at the Earth as a whole and seen how truly blessed it is with the types of delicious food that grows from its depths? The Earth itself is abound with the most succulent vegetables you will find, the juiciest fruits that you will find and the most nutritious grains you will find anywhere. Is it no wonder many people out there wonder why humans don't eat more food that grows from the Earth.

This particular class of food has been proven to be not only the healthiest food that we humans can eat, but its has been proven to be incredibly delicious, if made the right way.

What most people do not realize is what this diet can do not only to your physiological state, but your mental state as well. A Vegan diet enhances our physical body as well as your spiritual and emotional self as well. What does this mean? It pretty much means that you will live a much healthier, happier and much more peaceful life while on the Vegan diet.

So, what is a vegan?

A vegan is a person who permanently and strictly only consumes an all plant diet. Vegan is a person who not only consumes plant materials, but avoid all dietary or other products that derive from any living creature. A vegan usually does not believe that any animal, whether it is poultry, dairy or marine, should be harmed in the process of providing us with nourishment. To a vegan, all life is sacred, even those of animals and as such all life should be treated with the respect it deserves.

What Does A Vegan Diet Consist Of?

A true and organic vegan diet usually comprises of such foods such as fruits, seeds, nuts, legumes, grains and of course vegetables. Anything and everything that comes from the earth itself and can be grown in one's backyard is pretty much free game for a vegan.

The History of Veganism

The whole concept of both a vegetarian and a vegan diet is a much wider issue than many people realize. It is not just about eating a healthier diet and living a much healthier life. It goes deeper than that and its roots can be traced back to the very dawn of time for every human on the planet.

If you want to see exactly where a Vegan diet was born, you need to look back to the very birth of humanity itself and you can find a variety of history books on the subject matter.

The point of the matter is that no matter what a person is only as mentally, physically and emotionally healthy as the food they consume. The healthier the food, the healthier the person. It is that simple.

Chapter Two: How The Vegan Diet Can Protect You From Heart Disease and Stroke

The heart is the most important organ in the body today. Think about it, can you really live without your heart? However, as important as this organ is, it is still surprising that many people do not take special care of it the way that they should. More people today die from heart attacks and strokes than they do from most cancers. The main cause for these heart attacks is not stress or a unhealthy family history. In fact, it has to do with what we eat.

How The Vegan Diet Can Help Protect Your Heart

Let's take a closer look at this for a second. When a waxy substance known as plaque begins to build up inside the walls of your coronary artery, you will begin to develop a dangerous condition known as atherosclerosis. Of course this is not something that happens over night. This dangerous plaque builds up over the course of many years and comes from two primary sources: grease and meat.

Over time the plaque will begin to line the walls of your arteries and once this condition reaches a dangerous level, the artery itself can rupture or if it is large enough it can block all blood flow to your heart. This is known as a true heart attack. This type of attack deprives your heart of the very thing it needs: oxygen. Once that happen the heart muscles begins to die and will continue to die unless the situation is reversed as fast as possible.

This condition has been occurring as far back as we can remember. In the 1960's scientists began to experiment to come with solutions to this problem. Instead of finding a "cure" for a heart attack they found an interesting connection between the consumption of meat and heart attacks. It was even written in the American Medical Association journal in 1961 that by following a vegetarian or vegan diet, people could reduce the risk of heart attacks and development of heart disease by up to 97%.

When you consume an all meat diet, you are consuming high levels of negative cholesterol and saturated fats. These substance are then deposited straight into the arteries of your heart where they build up dangerously over time. On the other hand, when you follow a vegan diet, you are consuming such a low level of cholesterol and saturated fats that practically nothing will build up in the arteries of your heart. The simple fact is that a vegan diet equals a strong and healthy heart.

You also have to keep in mind that a vegan diet is high in nutritious fiber, which can be found commonly in many vegetable sources, grains and legumes. Fiber is one substance that helps to keep your heart healthy as well as your entire digestive tract. A vegan diet is also high in Vitamin C and important antioxidants, which all help to sustain a healthy heart as well.

How The Vegan Diet Can Help Protect You From A Stroke

When you think of a stroke, think of it as a heart attack but in your brain instead. A stroke is essentially when a blood clot forms in an artery inside your brain, blocking all important oxygen from reaching that section in your brain. When this happens the cells within that particular part of the brain begins to die of, resulting in critical brain damage.

Regardless of where the damage begins to occur in the brain, this brain damage that is suffered is traumatic. There are many things that your brain is responsible for and that you may not be aware of when you do them such as controlling your memory, control the movement of your body or controlling your speech. To be honest, nothing about a stroke is fun and in severe cases people have been known to die from this kind of attack.

So, what causes a stroke? It all comes down to nutrition and how well you have been eating throughout your life. Taking in harmful substances such as cholesterol and saturated fats increases the risk of developing these harmful clots in your brain and the more you consume, the more likely you are to suffer a stroke in your lifetime.

How will a Vegan diet help combat this condition?

Well, a Vegan diet is filled with healthy and important nutrients such as essential fatty acids, anti-oxidants and important minerals. All of these things help make this diet anti-inflammatory, which can help to remove excess stress on your body in the long run. This can help create an environment that is highly conductive, meaning that it can help prevent the formation of harmful plaque and clots in the long run.

Chapter Three: How Can A Vegan Diet Help Boost Your Emotional and Mental State of Mind

When you look at how you feel emotion, feel desires and have feelings, you need to take a step back and look at yourself from a different perspective. When you look at these things you need to look at yourself as an astral self and your body is an astral body. This "astral" body is the invisible part of your body that surrounds you. While I know this makes it sound as if you are some crazy shroom trip, just bear with me.

How A Vegan Diet Boosts your Emotional State of Mind

Now, the more purer your astral body, the more refined your actual body is. This astral part of yourself is the instrument that helps to control your emotional energy and your emotional state of mind. This emotional energy helps to develop power within yourself and helps to bring out the true beauty and wisdom of your very soul.

When it comes to eating the food that you need, it is important to keep in mind that the finest parts of the food that you eat are consumed by your astral body and can actually refine its appearance around you and thus influence your very emotional and mental state as well.

When you eat a meat-only centered diet, it pollutes your astral body and even jeopardizes the relation between your astral self. The animals that are slaughtered to feed us humans often live in a constant state of fear. For some people they believe that fear still lingers in the meat that we consume and hence contaminates our astral selves. When you eat meat that is contaminated with fear, many people believe that you are more prone to experiencing those emotions as well as experiencing anxiety and sorry.

However, consuming a solely vegan diet helps to promote more positive emotions such as joy, happiness, a sense of calm and even love.

How A Vegan Diet Can Boost Your Mental State of Mind

Our minds are perhaps the most complex thing about us. Our minds are wrapped in a delicate structure and surrounded by a mental aura that is invisible to the naked eye. The main function of our minds is to serve as an eternal connection between the human body and our souls, not just to help our body functions normally on a daily basis.

Now when we consume food, the most delicate and finest pieces infiltrate our minds and aura, influencing our very thoughts and feelings. The fact of the matter is that whatever food we consume, no matter what it is, becomes a part of our very minds and influences the way we think and feel on a day-to-day basis.

When you eat a diet primarily consisting of meat, your mental state of mind becomes very sense and course, vibrating at a frequency that is very low. What does this all mean? It simply means that the meat pollutes your mind and can intoxicate it in a very negative way. It can sabotage any calm feelings that you may have, inhibit your responsiveness to a situation and even reduce the clarity of which you think.

Now, when you consume a diet consisting of primarily vegan ingredients, your mind becomes in tune with the very light of your true self. A vegan diet consists of pure and refined components, all associated with a healthy state of mind. A vegan diet can enhance the clarity of which you think, increase its effectiveness and render your mind into an instrument that is as powerful as your human body. If you want a clear and calm mental state of mind, eating only a pure and healthy vegan diet is the way to go.

Chapter Four: The Other Benefits of Becoming An Awesome Vegan

There are many reasons why people decide to go Vegan and each person has their own story to tell about their journey to Veganism. However, there is one thing that every Vegan shares in common and that is the awesome benefits they are reaping while on this diet together.

There are three primary reasons why many people choose to adopt a Vegan lifestyle, but they are in no way the only reasons. These three popular reasons include:

1. Wanting To Be Fair To Animals

Being on a Vegan diet means that a person will not consume any food item that is of animal origin and they will not use any products that originate from animals. This means that Vegan will not touch dairy or egg products, even though these items do not kill the animal in the process or even use leather if it comes from an animal.

Many Vegans and people believe that animals should be able to exist on our planet, without interference from humans. Because of this reasoning many Vegans would rather sacrifice delicious meats and products for the good of animals and are happy doing so.

2. Wanting To Help The Environment

It is no secret that our planet has taken years and years of abuse from humans. Whether it is from global warming or harming our ozone layer, we are slowly destroying our planet. Because of this many Vegans believe that animal farming is something that is completely inefficient. The reason they believe this is because animal feed productions takes up a lot of land, water and resources that could be better spent helping our planet rather than destroying one of its inhabitants.

One of the most popular beliefs of Vegans who share this point of view is that investing in these livestock farms is the primary reason most of the earth's topsoil is eroding. Without this important topsoil, we are not able to cultivate our crops. In all reality the entire earth's population could be fed on the land we currently have if only the entire population became Vegan.

3. Want To Improve Their Overall Health

It is no secret that meat and fat has had a proven track record of doing more harm to a person's body then good. Consuming animal fats and animal protein have been linked to the development of diabetes, heart disease, cancer, high blood pressure, arthritis and various other medical ailments. There have also been numerous studies conducted that have shown meat eaters are also most likely to die prematurely then those that consume only plant based items.

Why is this? It is simply because our bodies are not designed to digest cow's milk, animal meat and the numerous types of animal fat out there. There have been numerous studies down that have found that people who solely consume plant based diets are either able to minimize the risk of developing chronic illnesses or they are able to live a much longer and healthy life in the long run.

What Are The Risks?

Surprisingly there is only one risk to becoming Vegan and it is one that many Vegans are not aware of prior to starting their new lifestyle. One of the things that Vegans will have to be wary of is Vitamin B12 Deficiency. The reason why this is so common among Vegans is because our bodies cannot use the plant form of this vitamin and so we cannot get an adequate amount into our bodies on a daily basis. Since this is very common among Vegans today it is extremely important that Vegans use a Vitamin B12 supplement on a daily basis to prevent this from happening.

Chapter Five: The Common Diseases That Affect Animals Today

Now, there are many disease that affect many animals today and that could end up in the meat that you consume. Many of these diseases have ended up in the news and it is surprising that even knowing the dangers that meat poses why people still continue to eat meat.

The Most Common Disease In Cattle Today

Anaplasmosis

This disease is one that affects the red blood cells in cattle and that comes from a parasite.

Once the parasite affects the red blood cells the cattle is more at risk to developing anemia, weight loss, fever, jerky movements, short of breath and in severe cases it can cause death.

Within 4 days of being diagnosed with these disease, cattle can go down one of two paths: Recovery or death. The death of an animal depends on their age and the older the animal the more likely they are to die from this disease.

Anthrax

This is one of the most popular and most heard of disease today as it scared an entire nation in 2001. This highly infectious and highly fatal disease is cause by a bacteria known as Bacillus anthracis.

Most of the animals that die from this disease often die in outbreaks that occur in the same area. This is because the spores that come from this bacteria remain live and active for many decades. This disease has been known to cause fever, depression, weakness and bloody discharges.

Bangs Disease

This disease is commonly known as the "Contagious Abortion." This infection comes from a bacteria known as Bucella and it is most commonly known to cause abortions or premature births in cattle.

The worst part about this organism is that it has been found in many products that we buy today such as milk and meat from dairy and meat cattle. When people consume it this organism causes what is known as Undulant Fever and becomes a public health hazard if it is not contained within a respectable amount of time.

The Most Common Disease In Chickens Today

There are 3 types of common diseases that affect chickens today and that can spread to the meat to contaminate it.

Nutritional Diseases

There are many different nutritional disease that affect chickens today. These diseases have been known to cause genetic defects and even impaired vision if left untreated. These diseases are usually caused by inadequate nutritional standards and if the chickens were fed appropriately at slaughterhouses or farms, these diseases could easily be stopped dead in their tracks.

Some of the most common types of nutritional diseases are Perosis, Cage Layer Fatigue and Fatty Liver Syndrome.

Infectious Diseases

The many types of infectious disease that spread among chickens today are primarily due to the fact that many of these animals are crammed into tiny cages and are within a few inches of each other. When one chicken becomes sick, the rest within the room are more likely to become sick as well.

Some of the most common types of infectious diseases that affect chickens today are Chicken Anemia Virus, The Avian Influenza, Fowl Pox, Mycoplasmosis, Infectious Bronchitis and Egg Drop Syndrome.

Parasitic Diseases

These types of diseases that affect chicken come from a variety of different parasites. Unfortunately and as sad as it may be chickens on farms and in slaughter houses do not have access to vets as often as they need and they are most likely to be riddled with parasites.

Some of the parasitic infections that affect chickens today are Lice, Toxoplasmosis and Coccidiosis.

The Most Common Diseases In Pigs Today

There are numerous different diseases that can affect pigs today and that can be transmitted to the food that we eat. Some of the diseases that can affect pigs today are Piglet anemia, Swine dysentery, Leptospirosis and Pneumonia.

With the variety of diseases that can affect farm animals today, it is almost next to impossible to guarantee that the meat that you consume is even safe at all. The truth of the matter is that no matter what, there is always a risk of contracting a harmful disease when you eat meat. So, why take the risk at all? Is it even worth it to become sick just to enjoy a burger?

Chapter Six: Helpful Tips To Becoming An Awesome Vegan

Starting something new can be both exciting and very scary all at the same time. However, there are a few things that many Vegans should all know and consider before fully committing to this lifestyle and in this chapter you will learn for yourself what helpful tips you will need in order to be a successful Vegan.

1. Have An Open Mind

There is no way faster to failure than having a certain way of negative thinking and attitude towards your new diet. This cannot be any truer for the Vegan diet and lifestyle and this is something that is not going to be easy for many people to commit to. Try to think very positive about this endeavor. If you go into it thinking that you are just punishing yourself and that it will not last forever, trust me it won't. That is the kind of thing that you want to avoid.

2. If Cooking At Home, Make Sure You Give Yourself Plenty of Time To Do So

There is nothing worse than making a fresh home cooked meal and having to rush through it. While it may seem like this is not going to be hard to do, arranging meals around vegetables will be a foreign concept for many people and it will take them several minutes to do and to get right the first time. Give yourself plenty of time to do this and you will be able to create hearty and delicious meals that will leave you feeling satisfied.

3. Avoid Any Type of Convenience Food

If you are skeptical about how delicious or savory vegan dishes can be, I highly recommend that you stay away from as many vegan convenience food products as possible.

Trust me, I have yet to taste one that has been good and that I liked really well. If you think that you will be able to live on frozen pizza, frozen vegan burritos and veggie burger patties every single day, you are going to be in one heck of a surprise.

4. Do Not Be Embarrassed About Living This Kind of Lifestyle

There may come a time where you will feel that you have to rationalize your decision or explain your decision to other people. You may even find yourself coming up with reasons behind your Vegan lifestyle such as, "I'm doing it as a research project or I didn't want to hurt animals." Regardless of what reason you are using, you will begin to notice the same thing happening over and over again: explaining yourself never feels good.

Never feel that you have to explain your decision to anybody. However, if you do want something to tell people I find it easy to come out and say, "I have always agreed with Vegan philosophy and this just felt right." Most people have nothing to say to that statement. In fact most people will become more intrigued and you will find yourself having an interesting discussion with people that you may or may not know.

5. If You Mess Up, Don't Beat Yourself Up Over It

Let's face it, none of us are perfect. There may be a couple of times when you may accidentally consume some butter with animal fat or accidentally had something with fish sauce in it. Unfortunately this happens more than you may like and if it happens to happen to you, do not beat yourself up about it.

If you are stuck somewhere whether it is your home or out on the road and you have no choice, but to consume something with a hint of animal in it then do it and do not beat

33

yourself up over it in the long run. You will have to make mistakes every now and then while on this diet and your time could be better spent learning from these mistakes then letting them hold you back.

6. Don't Be Afraid of The Produce Isle

Going Vegan means that you will get to become close and personal with the produce isle then you may have been before. Once you start this diet is a good idea to head down this isle to learn and explore exactly what your new diet will begin to consist of. Look at how much diversity you have with plants and try to come up with some creative meal ideas while surrounded by the main ingredients that you will be using.

7. Stay As Strong As You Possibly Can

Going Vegan is not the easiest thing that you will ever do. In fact, it will be one of the hardest things that you will do. The first few days will be especially tough on you, but I promise it does become easier as days pass. You will soon get into the swing of things and living this lifestyle will become easier and easier. It will come to a point that when you think of what you want to make for every meal, meat will never cross your mind.

8. There Are Plenty of Places To Eat Out At That Offer Healthy Vegan Options

Just because you are Vegan does not mean that you cannot indulge yourself on delicious food every once in a while. There are many restaurants that you can go to and till enjoy yourself such as Moe's Mexican restaurant, Johnny Rockets, Chipotle and P.F. Changs. If your friends ever want to go out and do something with you that involves eating, do not be afraid to suggest one of these popular restaurants.

9. Get On a Vitamin B12 Supplement

As discussed in the first chapter of this eBook, most Vegans tend to suffer from the same common ailment, which is Vitamin B12 deficiency. In order to reduce the risk of getting this ailment and to ensure that you feel as healthy as possible begin taking a Vitamin B12 supplement as soon as you begin this lifestyle. Trust me, you will not regret it in the long run.

10. When In Doubt, Stick With Simplicity

Just because you are a Vegan and you are using vegetables to make up the majority of your meals, it does not mean that you have to make the entire process complicated. The best recipes to make are the simple ones and not only will you enjoy these recipes, but so will your guests.

If you are just starting out on a Vegan Diet, these helpful tips will help you to become a successful Vegan in the long run. Whether you ensure to explore your options when eating out, staying as strong as possible with your new lifestyle, having an open mind about being a Vegan, making sure that you stay clear of Vegan convenience foods and making sure to give yourself plenty of time to prepare your meals, make sure that you try to follow these tips every once in a while. You will become a better Vegan for it in the long run.

Chapter Seven: Ways To Make Your Meals Taste Orgasmic!

When it comes to eating a Vegan diet most of the time people are hesitant about it. Why is this? The main reason people are resistant to the idea of eating a healthy Vegan diet is because many people are under the misconception that the food will not taste as good as a burger and fries will. This is one of the most popular misconceptions regarding a Vegan diet today and in my opinion it is one that stops many people from becoming great Vegans and from living a healthier lifestyle in the long run.

When you first begin preparing Vegan food, many people do not know how to make their dishes tastes good. There are so many different flavors to work with that bringing them out so that you can savor them can be extremely difficult. There are many different seasoning that you can use to bring out the flavor of your dish and to help impress not only yourself, but your friends and family as well.

Here are 5 different tips that you can use to help make your vegan meals taste more amazing and to get you excited to prepare your meals on a daily basis.

1. Make Sure That You Use Only High-Quality and Fresh Ingredients

One of the best ways to ensure that your food tastes just as delicious as possible is to ensure that you are using the highest quality ingredients that you can afford and that you are as fresh as possible.

If you are the type of person who usually only spends enough money to get the cheapest ingredients possible, you will begin to notice that you meals are lacking in flavor, making it more possible that you will stop your Vegan diet before you want to.

I highly recommend using fresh organic ingredients, as they always tend to pack more punch then ordinary produce. Keep in mind, the ingredients that are simple and that are not stuffed with things like salt and sugar, have more flavor and will help your meals to taste delicious in the long run.

2. Don't Be Afraid To Spice Things Up

Using different herbs and spices should start becoming a regular part of your meal preparing process and it is something that you should get in the habit of adding into your meals on a daily basis. Not only do herbs and spices help to add incredible flavor to your meals, but many of them are packed with important nutrients that your body needs on a daily basis.

Some of the most popular and great tasting spices that you can use are turmeric, cinnamon, cumin and ginger. These four spices can help liven up a dull vegan dish and can even help benefit your body in the long run such as by giving your digestive system a boost that it desperately needs.

Using fresh herbs in your dishes can also help give your body important antioxidants and nutrients that it needs. Herbs like Parsley, cilantro, Basil and Mint can be used for much more then great tasting garnishes and you can use them for a variety of reasons in your main dishes.

3. When Using Beans and Grains, Give Them A Boost Once In A While

If you have ever eaten plain chickpeas or brown rice, you know better than anybody how unappealing they can be. They are completely bland and don't really have much of a taste to them. If you are making a dish that must incorporate these two ingredients, I highly recommend that you do not serve them on their own.

I highly recommend pairing your beans and grains with ingredients that are rich in flavor. Try mixing them with some of your favorite pieces of fruit. There are even some vegetables that you can use that can help liven up the flavors of these otherwise bland foods.

I also recommend adding a healthy helping of flavorful sauce or dressing to some of these ingredients.

4. Don't Be Afraid To Use Fat In Your Meals

While choosing the right kind of fat to use in your dish is important to keep your meals and yourself as healthy as possible, the more you do it, the easier the process becomes down the line. Adding healthy forms of fat not only have healthy benefits for you, but it can go a long way into making your meals much more delicious. Fat carries the richness of the entire dish and can make or break how the dish will taste to you and your family.

There are many types of healthy fat that you can use to enhance the flavor of your dish such as fats coming from whole foods like seeds, avocados, olives and nuts. If you find that you are preparing a meal for other people who are following the Vegan lifestyle as well, it will help to add a healthy form of fat to enhance the taste of dish.

5. Don't Be Afraid To Use Salt Here and There

Salt helps out to bring out the flavor of important vegan ingredients such as vegetables and even helps to soften them a bit whenever you are cooking them up or sautéing them.

When you are preparing your meals do not be afraid to add as much salt as you want to help bring out the flavor of your veggies.

If you are afraid of taking in too much sodium there are healthy alternatives that you can use to help enhance the flavor of your dishes. Don't be afraid to use vegetable salt every once in a while as it contains lots of important nutrients and less sodium than regular table salt.

I know that starting a Vegan diet can be very scary and can even feel intimidating when you do not believe that you will be able to eat delicious meals again. However, there are certain things that you can do to enhance the flavors of your dishes such as using salt, healthy forms of fat or using fruits to bring out the flavors of your dishes. Follow these helpful tips to make the most delicious Vegan recipes you will ever make in your life.

Vegan Breakfast Recipes

Lemon Scones Vegan Style

This delicious recipe is one that every Vegan should try. With this recipe you can feel free to be as creative as you want and you can experiment as much as you like as well.

Total Prep Time: 25 Minutes

Serves: 12

Ingredients:

-¾ Cup of Sugar, White

-4 tsp. of Baking Powder

-½ tsp. Salt

-¾ Cup of Margarine, Slightly Melted

-2 Cups of Flour, All Purpose

-½ Cup of Water

-2 Tbsp. of Poppy Seeds

-1 Lemon, Used For Juice and Zest

-½ Cup of Soy Milk

Directions:

1. Preheat your oven to 400 degrees. While it heats up grease a small baking sheet and set aside.

2. In a large mixing bowl combine your sugar, flour, salt and baking powder until thoroughly combined. Add in your margarine and cut it into your mixture until it has the consistency of sand. Then stir in your lemon juice, poppy seeds and lemon zest.

3. Next add in your soymilk and water together and stir with your dry ingredients until your mixture slowly becomes a batter that is thick. It should resemble biscuit dough.

4. Then spoon small amounts of your dough onto your greased baking sheet and ensure that your scones are about 3 inches apart from each other.

5. Place Into Your Oven and bake for the next 10 to 15 minutes until they are golden brown in color. Remove from oven and place on cooling rack to cool before serving.

Blueberry and Cornmeal Pancakes

When you make these pancakes, you will never have to worry about breaking your vegan diet at all. These pancakes tastes extremely great with some warmed blueberry jam or your favorite brand of syrup.

Total Prep Time: 25 Minutes

Serves: 4

Ingredients:

-1 Cup of Soymilk

-¼ tsp. of Salt For Taste

-1 Cup of Flour, Whole Wheat

-½ Cup of Water

-1 tsp. of Baking Powder

-½ tsp. of Baking Soda

-1 Cup of Blueberries, Fresh

-2 Tbsp. of Vegetable Oil

-½ Cup of Cornmeal, Ground

Directions:

1. Preheat your oven to 200 degrees. While it heats up take out a small mixing bowl and combine your water and soy milk into it.

2. In a separate mixing bowl combine your dry ingredients together: baking powder, flour,

baking soda, flour and salt until all ingredients are thoroughly mixed. Then stir in your soymilk and water mixture to your dry ingredients. As you continue to stir fold in your fresh blueberries gently and stir until well mixed. Allow your batter to sit for at least 5 minutes.

3. Grab a skillet and lightly grease it with a generous amount of cooking spray. Heat it over medium heat and then pour about ¼ cup of batter into your skillet. Cook gently until bubbles begin to form on the top of your pancake and flip it. Allow to cook on the other side for about 3 to 5 minutes. Remove from skillet and place on a baking sheet. Place the baking sheet into your oven and allow your pancakes to remain warm while you cook the rest of your batter.

Vegan Style Crepes

Crepes are absolutely delicious and many people who are on a vegan diet often wonder if they can even enjoy this excellent breakfast dish. Well, now you no longer need to worry as this crepe recipe has a classic vegan style twist on it. Not only will this recipe taste great, but it will leave you wanting more.

Total Prep Time: 2 ½ Hours

Serves: 4

Ingredients:

-½ Cup of Water

-1 Tbsp. of Sugar, Turbinado

-½ Cup of Soymilk

-¼ tsp. of Salt, For Taste

-2 Tbsp. of Syrup

-1 Cup of Flour, Unbleached and All Purpose

-¼ Cup of Soy Margarine, Melted

Directions:

1. In a large mixing bowl combine your soymilk, water, syrup, salt, margarine and water together until thoroughly mixed. Cover your mixture with some plastic wrap and allow to chill in your refrigerate for at least 2 hours.

2. Take out a medium sized skillet and lightly grease it with some soy margarine over medium to high heat. Pour about 3 Tbsp. of your chilled batter into your skillet and swirl around to ensure your batter covers the entire bottom of the skillet. Cook your crepe until golden in color an flip to cook on the opposite side.

Breakfast Style Raisin and Rice Pudding

With this recipe you can finally find a way to put your leftover rice to good use. Feel free to serve this dish while hot or cold. Either way it will taste great.

Total Prep Time: 20 Minutes

Serves: 4

Ingredients:

-1 Cup of Soymilk

-1 Cup of Water

-½ Cup of Raisins

-¼ Cup of Syrup Of Your Choice

-1 tsp. of Cinnamon, Ground

-½ Cup of Almonds, Toasted and Chopped Finely

-3 Cups of Brown Rice, Fully Cooked

-½ tsp. of Cardamom, Ground

Directions:

1. In a small mixing bowl combine your raisins, soymilk, cardamom, cooked rice, chopped almonds, syrup and cinnamon. Place into a pot over medium to high heat and allow to come to a boil.

2. Once it comes to a boil reduce the heat to low and allow your pudding to simmer for the next 5 to 8 minutes. Remove from heat and serve into small bowls.

Breakfast Strawberry and Oatmeal Smoothie

This rich vegan smoothie is extremely filling and will surely satisfy any food cravings that you may have. It is pink in color and contains a creamy texture that will leave you wanting more.

Total Prep Time: 5 Minutes

Serves: 2

Ingredients:

-1 Cup of Milk, Soy

-14 Strawberries, Fresh or Frozen

-½ tsp. of Vanilla Extract

-½ Cup of Oats, Rolled

-1 ½ tsp. of Sugar, White

-1 Banana, Peeled and Cut Into Small Chunks

Directions:

1. In a blender, combine all of your ingredients together and blend on the lowest setting until if reaches the desired consistency. Pour into small glasses and serve immediately.

Vegan Style Apple and Carrot Breakfast Muffins

This is the perfect recipe to make if you want to impress your family or friends at the office. This recipe makes plenty of muffins that are incredibly delicious and that are healthy for you.

Total Prep Time: 40 Minutes

Serves: 12

Ingredients:

-1 Cup of Brown Sugar

-4 tsp. of Cinnamon, Ground

-½ Cup of Sugar, White

-1 tsp. of Baking Powder

-2 ½ Cups of Flour, All-Purpose

-4 tsp. of Baking Soda

-6 tsp. of Egg Replacer, Dry

-2 tsp. of Salt

-¼ Cup of Vegetable Oil

-2 Cups of Carrots, Finely Grated

-2 Apples, Large In Size, Peeled, Cored and Shredded Finely

-1 ¼ Cups of Applesauce

Directions:

1. Preheat your oven to 375 degrees. As it heats up grease a muffin tin lightly or line it some muffin liners

2. In a large sized mixing bowl combine your baking soda, white sugar, cinnamon, brown sugar, flour, salt and baking powder together and stir until all of the ingredients are thoroughly combined.

3. In a small sized mixing bowl whisk together

your applesauce, oil and dry egg substitute until all of the ingredients are mixed completely. Then stir this into your dry ingredients until thoroughly mixed.

4. Spoon some batter generously into your greased muffin pan at least ¾ of the way full for each muffin tin.

5. Place into your oven and bake for the next 20 minutes. Remove from oven and allow your muffins to cool for about 5 minutes before trying to remove your muffins from the pan.

Healthy Banana and Kale Smoothie

This smoothie is rich in important nutrients that your body craves on a daily basis. While it does contain kale, the flavor of the banana hides it completely, leaving you with a smoothie that you will simple love.

Total Prep Time: 5 Minutes

Serves: 1

Ingredients:

-1 Banana, Peeled and Cut Into Small Chunks

-2 Cups of Kale, Chopped

-1 Tbsp. of Flaxseeds

-1 tsp. of Syrup, Maple

-½ Cup of Soymilk, Unsweetened and Light

Directions:

1. Place all over your ingredients into a blender and blend until the smoothie reaches the consistency that you like. Pour into a drinking glass and serve immediately.

Classic Oat Bran Cereal

If you need a dish that you can make fast and that is relatively easy to make, this is the perfect recipe for you. This hot breakfast recipe is sweetened with sugar substitute and some dried plums, making it a nutritious and delicious recipe.

Total Prep Time: 10 Minutes

Serves: 1

Ingredients:

-1 Cup of Water, Warm

-5 Dried Prunes, Chopped Into Small Pieces

-¼ Cup of Oat Bran

-¼ tsp. of Cinnamon, Ground

-1 tsp. of Sugar Substitute, Splenda

Directions:

1. In a small to medium sized saucepan, combine your prunes, splenda, water and cinnamon together. Heat over low to medium heat until it reaches a boil.

2. Then stir in your oat bran and allow to boil for the next 2 minutes. Remove from heat and serve immediately.

Vegan Lunch Recipes

Spicy Lentil Wraps

A great recipe to help wake you up right in the middle of the day. This dish is really easy to make and will leave you feeling full for the rest of the day.

Total Prep Time: 60 Minutes

Serves: 6

Ingredients For Wraps:

-2 Cups of Water, Warm

-¾ Cups of Bulgur, Fine Grain

-½ Cup of Lentils, Red and Rinsed

-2 tsp. of Cumin, Ground

-2 Tbsp. of Olive Oil

-½ tsp. of Salt

-1 Scallion, Chopped Finely

-1 tsp. of Red Pepper Flakes

-2 Cubs of Cabbage, Shredded

-2 Tbsp. of Parsley, Fresh and Finely Chopped

-¾ Cup of Red Pepper Paste

-6 Sheet of Lavish, Whole Wheat or White

Ingredients For Tahini Sauce:

-¼ Cup of Tahini

-2 tsp. of Lemon Juice, Fresh

-¼ tsp. of Garlic, Crushed

-1/8 tsp. of Salt

-2/3 Cup of Warm Water

-1/8 tsp. of Red Pepper Flakes

-2 tsp. of Parsley, Fresh and Finely Chopped

Directions For Wraps:

1. In a small saucepan over medium heat, combine both your lentils and your water together. Allow the water to boil then reduce the water to a small simmer. Allow your lentils to simmer for about 20 minutes or until they become soft.

2. Remove from heat and stir in your bulgur and all to sit with your water and lentils for about 30 minutes or until it becomes soft.

3. While the bulgur sits, heat some oil in a medium sized saucepan. Sauté your onions, red pepper flakes and cumin together until the onions are translucent. Once soft add this mixture to your bulgur mixture and stir until all of the ingredients are thoroughly combined.

4. To assemble lay out one sheet of lavish and put together like a burrito. Wait to wrap it up until the tahini sauce.

Directions For Tahini Sauce:

1. In a small sized mixing combine all of your ingredients together and stir with a form until all of the ingredients are combined thoroughly.

2. Then gradually add some warm water to it until the sauce reaches the consistency that you are looking for and serve about 1 Tbsp. with your lentil wraps.

Delicious Quinoa Salad With Fresh Avocado and Dill

What lunch is completely without a salad. If you haven't gotten the chance to try Quinoa yet, this recipe will help you fall in love with it. Feel free to be creative as you want with this recipe and add in whatever additional vegan friendly ingredients that you want.

Total Prep Time: 30 Minutes

Serves: 4 to 6

Ingredients:

-1 Cup of Quinoa, Golden

-1 Shallot, Large In Size and Chopped Finely

-1 ¾ Cups of Vegetable Broth

-8 Radishes, Small In Size and Chopped Finely

-2/3 Cups of Dill, Stems Gone

-3 Tbsp. of Olive Oil, Extra Virgin

-½ Tbsp. of Vinegar, Balsamic

-½ Cup of Almonds, Sliced Finely

-½ Cup of Dates, Chopped Roughly

-½ Lemon, Fresh and Used From Juice and Zest

-1/3 of a Cucumber, Sliced Thinly

-Dash of Salt and Pepper For Taste

-1 Avocado, Ripe and Cut Into Small Chunks

Directions:

1. Rinse your quinoa while using a fine mesh strainer for at least 2 to 3 minutes, making sure to rub the quinoa vigorously while you are doing it.

2. In a medium sized saucepan heat up your extra virgin olive oil and cook your quinoa in the oil for about 1 to 2 minutes. Then pour in your vegetable broth and allow to come to a boil. Once it does turn the heat down to the lowest setting and allow to cook for about 15 minutes. After 15 minutes remove from heat and allow to sit for 5 minutes.

3. Drain your quinoa and place into a bowl to allow to cool completely.

4. Place your remaining ingredients into a

small sized mixing bowl and toss until all of the ingredients are thoroughly combined. Toss in your quinoa and stir until well mixed.

5. Serve into a salad bowl and enjoy immediately.

Vegan Style Mac and Cheese

Nobody said that even as a vegan, you cannot enjoy mac and cheese every once in a while. Even though cheese is definitely on the list of things that you naturally can't have, this recipe will leave you a dish that you will certainly crave on a daily basis.

Total Prep Time: 1 Hour and 15 Minutes

Serves: 4

Ingredients:

-3 Tbsp. of Yeast, Nutritional Kind

-1 Pack of Macaroni, Elbow Kind and Uncooked

-1 Onion, Medium In Size, Finely Chopped

-1 Tbsp. of Vegetable Oil

-1/3 Cup of Lemon Juice, Fresh

-1 1/3 Cups of Warm Water

-1 Cup of Cashews, Finely Chopped

-1/3 Cup of Canola Oil

-Dash of Salt and Pepper For Taste

-1 tsp. of Garlic Powder

-1 tsp. of Onion Powder

-4 Ounces of Red Peppers, Roasted and Drained

Directions:

1. Preheat your oven to 350 degrees.

2. While your oven heats up, cook up your elbow macaroni until it is al dente. Once your

drain it transfer it to a medium sized baking dish.

3. In a medium sized saucepan, sauté your onions over low to medium heat or until they are softened and lightly brown in color. Remove from heat and mix in with your macaroni in the baking dish.

4. Using a food processor put your lemon juice, cashews, salt and some water and mix up until it reaches a fine consistency. Then toss in the remainder of your ingredients and blend until smooth. Pour this in with your macaroni and onions and stir until all of the ingredients are mixed well.

5. Place into your oven and bake for 45 minutes until your macaroni is lightly brown. Remove from your oven and allow to cool for at least 10 to 15 minutes before you serve it.

Hearty Zucchini and Red Pepper Stew

This dish will satisfy you unlike any other vegan dish that you come across. It is hearty and savory, making this a dish that you will want to make all of the time.

Total Prep Time: 1 Hour and 20 Minutes

Serves: 4 Servings

Ingredients:

-¼ Cup of Olive Oil

-½ Cup of Rice, Basmati

-1 Eggplant, Sliced Into 1 Inch Cubes

-5 Cloves of Garlic, Chopped Finely

-3 Tomatoes, Fresh and Diced Into Small Pieces

-1 Cup of Onions, Chopped Finely

-1 Red Bell pepper, Chopped Into Small Pieces

-1 ½ Cups of Water, Warm

-¼ tsp. of Red Pepper Flakes

-¼ Cup of Basil, Fresh

-½ tsp. of Salt and Pepper For Taste

-¼ Cup of Parsley, Fresh and Chopped Finely

-1 Sprig of Rosemary, Fresh and Chopped

-1 Cup of Wine, Marsala

Directions:

1. Place your eggplant into a medium sized colander and sprinkle with your dash of salt and pepper. Slice up your eggplant and sauté in a pan with some oil until it is slightly brown in color. Then stir in your onion and sauté until the onions are translucent. Next add in your garlic and sauté with your eggplant and onion for about 2 to 3 minutes.

2. Then stir in your rice, tomatoes, water, red pepper flakes, some additional salt, pepper, zucchini and red bell pepper. Make sure your cook your mixture over medium heat until it reaches a nice rolling boil and then reduce the heat. Allow to simmer for about 45 minutes or until all of your vegetables are tender.

3. Remove from heat and stir in your rosemary, basil and parsley until thoroughly combined. Serve while still piping hot.

Vegan Style Black Bean Quesadillas

These quesadillas pack quite a punch and will leave you feel exceptionally full. You can gorge all your want without feeling guilty about consuming cheese.

Total Prep Time: 55 Minutes

Serves: 4

Ingredients:

-1 Clove of Garlic, Minced

-1 Can of Northern Beans, Drained and Rinsed Prior to Use

-¼ tsp. of Chili Powder

-¾ Cup of Tomatoes, Diced

-1 tsp. of Cumin, Ground

-1/3 Cup of Yeast, Nutritional

-¼ Cup of Tomatoes, Diced Finely

-1 Pinch of Cayenne Pepper

-1 Tbsp. of Olive Oil

-Some Cooking Spray

-8 Tortillas, Whole Grain

-½ Cup of Vegan Black Beans, Drained and Rinsed

-Dash of Salt and Pepper For Tastes

Directions:

1. Using a food processor blend up your Northern beans, garlic and ¾ cup of diced tomatoes until it reaches a smooth consistency. Then add in your cumin, salt, pepper, chili powder, red pepper flakes and nutritional yeast until thoroughly mixed and smooth.

2. Transfer your mixture to a bowl and then stir in your black beans and ¼ cup of diced Tomatoes. Stir until thoroughly mixed.

3. Heat some olive oil over medium heat in a medium sized saucepan. Place one tortilla into your saucepan and fill the middle with a generous amount of bean filling. Place a second tortilla on top of your filling and allow to cook for about 10 minutes.

4. Spray the top of your quesadilla with some cooking spray and flip to allow to cook on the

other side for about 6 to 7 minutes. Slide onto a plate and serve immediately.

Scrambled Up Tofu

If you are looking to enjoy a high protein meal to help bring some enjoyment in your day, you are going to love this recipe. Feel free to add spinach, cashews or mushrooms to this dish as a topping.

Total Prep Time: 25 Minutes

Serves: 4

Ingredients:

-1 Onion, Medium In Size and Chopped Finely

-1 Tbsp. of Olive Oil

-3 Cloves of Garlic, Minced

-½ Can of Black Olives, Drained and Cut Into halves

-1 Pack of Tofu, Drained and Cut Into Cubes

-1 Tbsp. of Soy Sauce

-3 Tbsp. of Yeast, Nutritional

Directions:

1. Using a cast iron skillet, heat up some oil over low to medium heat, cook your onion until they are softened. This should take about 5 to 10 minutes. Then add in your tofu, olives and garlic. Cover your skillet and allow to cook for an additional 8 minutes, stirring every once in a while.

2. Then add in your yeast and soy sauces. Stir until your yeast fully dissolves which should take about 1 to 2 minutes.

Asian Style Lettuce Wraps

This dish is packed with delicious veggies,

crunchy vegetables and fresh ginger. This dish is not only very colorful, but it tastes great as well.

Total Prep Time: 22 Minutes

Serves: 8 Wraps

Ingredients:

-2 tsp. of Canola Oil

-1 Clove of Garlic, Minced

-2 Tbsp. of Hoisin Sauce

-1 Pinch of Red Chili Peppers, Dried

-2 tsp. of Gingerroot, Grated Finely

-1/2 tsp. of Sesame Oil

-A few Leaves of Lettuce

-1/3 Cup of Coriander, Fresh and Chopped Finely

-1/3 Cup of Green Onion, Chopped Finely

-½ Cup of Cucumber, Diced Into Thin Pieces

-½ Cup of Carrot, Shredded

-½ Cup of Red Pepper, Sweet and Diced Into Small Pieces

Directions:

1. In a large sized non-stick skillet, heat up some oil over low to medium heat. Add in your garlic and gingerroot and allow to cook for the next 2 minutes or until they become soft and light brown in color.

2. Next stir in your sesame oil and hoisin sauce. Add in your chili peppers and stir until well mixed. Reduce your heat to the lowest setting and cook for the next 5 minutes.

3. Remove from heat and lay out your lettuce wraps on a flat surface. Take about 3 Tbsp. of your vegetable filling onto each leaf of lettuce and wrap like a burrito. Enjoy.

Classic Chickpea Curry

While this is an easy recipe to make, it allows you to be as creative as you want with it. Do not hesitate to spice up the ingredients a bit especially if you usually make this dish as frequently as possible.

Total Prep Time: 40 Minutes

Serves: 8

Ingredients:

-2 Onions, Minced

-2 Tbsp. of Vegetable Oil

-1 tsp. of Cumin, Ground

-6 Cloves, Whole

-2 Cloves of Garlic, Minced

-1 tsp. of Coriander, Ground

-Dash of Salt and Pepper For Taste

-1 Cup of Cilantro, Fresh

-1 tsp. of Cayenne Pepper

-1 tsp. of Turmeric, Ground

-2, 15 Ounce Cans of Garbanzo Beans

-2 Sticks of Cinnamon, Crushed

-2 tsp. of Ginger Root, Fresh and Chopped Finely

Directions:

1. Using a large frying pan, heat up some oil in it and fry your onions until they are tender.

2. Stir in the remainder of your ingredients and allow to cook for about 30 to 35 minutes. Remove from heat and stir in your cilantro just before serving. Enjoy.

Vegan Dinner Recipes

Vegan Style Fajitas

This recipe is the most wonderful version of meatless fajitas that you can make. It make enough that you can prepare it ahead of time or save a little extra for your friends and family.

Total Prep Time: 1 Hour and 10 Minutes

Serves: 6

Ingredients:

-¼ Cup of Vinegar, Red Wine

-1 tsp. of Sugar, White

-¼ Cup of Olive Oil

-1 tsp. of Chili Powder

-1 tsp. of Oregano, Dried

-Dash of Salt, Garlic Salt and Pepper For Taste

-2 Zucchini, Small In Size and Slice Julienne Style

-1 Onion, Large In Size, Sliced Into Small Pieces

-1 Yellow Squash, Small In Size and Sliced Julienne Style

-2 Tbsp. of Olive Oil

-1, 15 Ounce Can of Black Beans, Drained and Rinsed

-1, 8 Ounce Can of Corn, Whole Kernel and Drained

-1 Red Bell Pepper, Cut Into Thin Strips

-1 Green Bell Pepper, Cut Into Thin Strips

Directions:

1. In a medium sized mixing bowl combine your oregano, garlic salt, salt, sugar, pepper,

olive oil, vinegar and chili powder until well mixed. Then add in your onion, squash and peppers to the marinade and stir until thoroughly mixed. Place in your fridge for at least 30 minutes.

2. Heat up a large sized skillet over low to medium heat. Add in your drained vegetables and sauté all of them until they are tender. This should take about 10 to 15 minutes. Then stir in your beans and corn and cook over high heat for at least 5 minutes. Serve while still piping hot.

Vegan Style Spicy Potato Curry

If you have ever been bored of curry, this recipe will change your mind. This recipe helps to bring a little spice and flavor into a traditional curry dish that you will fall in love with.

Total Prep Time: 60 Minutes

Serves: 6

Ingredients:

-4 tsp. of Curry Powder

-4 Potatoes, Washed, Peeled and Cut Into Small Cubes

-2 Tbsp. of Vegetable Oil

-3 Cloves of Garlic, Minced

-1 ½ tsp. of Cayenne Pepper

-1 Onion, Yellow In Color and Diced Into Small Chunks

-2 tsp. of Cumin, Ground

-2 tsp. of Salt

-4 tsp. of Garam Masala

-1 Ginger Root, Peeled and Minced

-1, 14 Ounce Can of Tomatoes, Diced Into Small Chunks

-1, 14 Ounce Can of Coconut Milk

-1, 15 Ounce Can of Peas, Drained

-1, 15 Ounce Can of Chickpeas, Drained and Rinsed

Directions:

1. Place your potatoes into a large sized pot over high heat. Place some salt into it with your potatoes and allow your potatoes to boil for about 15 minutes or until they become tender. Drain your potatoes and let them dry out by themselves for about a minute or two.

2. Then using a large non-stick skillet, sauté your onions and garlic in some vegetable oil over medium heat. Sauté until the onions become translucent in color, which should take about 5 minutes. Then season your sautéed veggies with some curry powder, salt, ginger, garam masala, cumin and cayenne pepper.

3. Next add in your tomatoes, peas, potatoes, garbanzo beans and coconut milk and stir until thoroughly blended. Allow your mixture to simmer for 5 to 10 minutes and then serve while still piping hot.

Delicious Avocado Tacos

These tacos are simple and easy to make and taste amazing as well. You will want to make this dish all of the time.

Total Prep Time: 25 Minutes

Serves: 6

Ingredients:

-¼ Cup of Onions, Diced Into Small Pieces

-3 Avocados, Peeled, Pitted and Mashed Into A Smooth Consistency

-¼ tsp. of Garlic Salt

-Dash of Jalapeno Pepper Sauce, For Taste

-12 Corn Tortillas

-Some Fresh Leaves of Cilantro, Chopped Finely

Directions:

1. Preheat your oven to 325 degrees.

2. While your oven heats up, take out a medium sized mixing bowl. In the bowl mix up your garlic salt, avocado and onions until it reaches a smooth consistency.

3. Then arrange your tortillas on a greased baking sheet and place into your oven for 2 to 5 minutes so that they are heated through. Then spread your avocado mixture onto your tortillas and garnish with some fresh cilantro and jalapeno pepper sauce. Serve immediately.

Traditional Vegan Quinoa Chard Pilaf

This incredibly simple vegan dish combines a variety of delicious ingredients that you will surely love. It also is very colorful, which will surely even please the pickiest of eaters.

Total Prep Time: 40 Minutes

Serves: 8

Ingredients:

-1 Onion, Medium In Size and Diced Into Small Pieces

-1 Tbsp. of Olive Oil

-3 Cloves of Garlic, Minced

-2 Cups of Quinoa, Uncooked and Rinsed

-1 Quart of Vegetable Broth

-1 Cup of Lentils, Canned and Rinsed

-1 Bunch of Swiss Chard, Stems Cut

-8 Ounces of Mushrooms, Chopped Finely

Directions:

1. In a medium sized pan, heat up some oil over low to medium heat. Pour your chopped onion and garlic into the pan and sauté for about 5 minutes or until the onion becomes tender. Mix in your quinoa, mushrooms and lentils. Stir thoroughly until completely combined.

2. Next pour in your vegetable broth and cover. Allow to simmer for about 20 minutes.

3. Remove your pot from heat and gently mix in your Swiss chard. Cover again and let your mixture sit for 5 minutes or until it is fully wilted.

Vegan Style Shepherd's Pie

Even though following a Vegan diet can be tough, it does not mean that you can't still enjoy recipes you love. With this recipe you will be able to enjoy a meatless shepherd's pie that tastes great

Total Prep Time: 1 Hour and 15 Minutes

Serves: 8

Ingredients:

-Dash of Salt and Pepper For Taste

-2 Cups of Vegetable Broth, Divide Into 2, 1 Cup Servings

-½ Cup of Lentils, Dry

-1 Carrot, Large In Size and Diced Into Fine Pieces

-½ of an Onion, Chopped Finely

-¼ Cup of Barley, Pearl

-1 tsp. of Yeast Extract

-½ tsp. of Water

-3 Potatoes, Chopped Into Small Pieces

-½ Cup of Walnuts, Chopped Coarsely

-1 tsp. of Flour, All Purpose

Directions:

1. Preheat your oven to 350 degrees.

2. Using a large sized saucepan over low to medium heat add in your broth, lentils, barley and yeast extract and stir until mixed. Allow to simmer for about 30 minutes.

3. In a separate medium sized saucepan, bring together your vegetable broth, walnuts, onions and carrots and allow to cook until the vegetables are still tender. This should take about 15 minutes.

4. In another separate pot, bring some water and salt together and bring to a boil. Place your potatoes into this pot and allow them to cook over medium to high heat for 15 minutes or until they become tender. Once tender drain the potatoes and mashed them until they reach the consistency you want.

5. Add in your flour and water to your carrot mixture and stir until thoroughly combined. Combine your carrot mixture with your lentil mixture next and season with as much salt and pepper as you like. Pour this mixture into a baking dish and place into your oven for about 30 minutes or until the top is nice and brown. Remove from oven and serve while still piping hot.

Mediterranean Zucchini

If you are a fan of Mediterranean cuisine then you are going to love this recipe. Feel free to serve this dish over a side of rice or nutritious egg noodles to make the perfect dinner meal.

Total Prep Time: 60 Minutes

Serves: 6

Ingredients:

-3 Cloves of Garlic, Crushed and Minced

-2 Cups of Water

-3 Tbsp. of Olive Oil

-1 Red Bell Pepper, Finely Chopped

-1 Onion, Large In Size and Chopped Finely

-1 Cup of White Rice, Long Grain

-Dash of Salt and Pepper For Taste

-1, 14 Ounce Can of Tomatoes, Peeled and Chopped Finely

-3 Cups of Zucchini, Chopped Into Small Pieces

-½ tsp. of Oregano, Dried

-1, 15 Ounce Can of Cannellini Beans, Drained and Rinsed

Directions:

1. In a medium sized saucepan, bring some water oven medium heat and stir in your rice. Allow to simmer for about 20 minutes until it is fully cooked.

2. In another saucepan, heat up some oil over low to medium heat. Stir in your garlic, onion and red bell pepper. Stir consistently until the mixture becomes fully tender. Mix in your tomatoes and zucchini next. Season with some salt, pepper and oregano and cover your skillet. Reduce your heat and allow to simmer for the

next 20 minutes, making sure to stir as frequently as possible.

3. Then stir in your bean to your mixture and let cook for an additional 10 minutes. Once done serve over your cooked rice and enjoy.

Delicious Tomato Pasta

This is an extremely simple recipe to make and you will want to make it as frequently as possible. Feel free to use whatever kind of pasta that you like.

Total Prep Time: 22 Minutes

Serves: 2

Ingredients:

-1 Tomato, Medium In Size and Coarsely Chopped

-1 Clove of Garlic, Coarsely Chopped

-Dash of Salt and Pepper For Taste

-1 tsp. of Basil, Dried

-1 Tbsp. of Olive Oil

-1 Package of Pasta of Your Choice, Dried

Directions:

1. Cook your pasta thoroughly in a large pot of boiling water. Cook until pasta is al dente, drain and set aside to use later.

2. In a small mixing bowl combine your tomatoes, basil, olive oil and salt. Toss until all of the ingredients are thoroughly mixed. Pour over your cooked pasta and serve. Enjoy.

Teriyaki Style Tofu With Pineapple

You would be surprised by how well tofu and teriyaki work well together. This dish has a bit of spice and tang that you will fall in love with.

Total Prep Time: 1 Hour and 25 Minutes

Serves: 4

Ingredients:

-2 Cups of Teriyaki Sauce, Your Favorite Kind

-1 Pack of Tofu, Firm

-1 Cup of Pineapple, Fresh and Chopped Into Small Chunks

Directions:

1. Slice up your tofu until you have a bunch of bite sized pieces and place them into a baking dish. Add in your pineapple and teriyaki sauce and mix until the tofu is evenly coated. Place into your fridge for at least 1 hour.

2. Preheat your oven to 350 degrees and upon being chilled for an hour place your dish into your oven. Allow to bake for 20 minutes or

until the dish is piping hot and bubbly. Remove and serve immediately.

Vegan Desserts

Vegan Style Cupcakes

I know that giving up anything ingredient made from animals can be quite difficult at times, it is not at all impossible to enjoy great tasting desserts. This recipe will help you make the most delicious cupcakes you will ever make and they taste just like the real thing.

Total Prep Time: 25 Minutes

Serves: 18

Ingredients:

-1 Tbsp. of Vinegar, Apple Cider

-1 Cup of Sugar, White

-1 ½ Cups of Milk, Almond

-2 tsp. of Baking Powder

-1 ¼ tsp. of Vanilla Extract

-½ tsp. of Baking Soda

-2 Cups of Flour, All Purpose

-½ tsp. of Salt

-½ Cup of Coconut Oil, Warmed Up Until It Is A Liquid

Directions:

1. Preheat your oven to 350 degrees. While it heats up make sure to grease up to muffin pans with a generous amount of cooking spray or some muffin liners.

2. Using a large sized mixing bowl combine your dry ingredients and whisk together until mixed well. Using a separate mixing bowl combine all of your wet ingredients together and when you are ready pour into your dry ingredients. Stir until all of the ingredients are blended well together.

3. Spoon enough batter into your muffin pans so that each muffin tin is about ¾ full.

4. Place your muffin pans into your oven and bake for about 15 to 20 minutes or until the tops of the muffins spring back. Remove from oven and place on a cooling rack to cool off completely before your serve it.

Mouthwatering Tofu Pumpkin Pie

This recipe is a classic twist on your traditional pumpkin pie. Feel free to make this lighter in fat by using Splenda instead of half of your sugar.

Total Prep Time: 2 Hours

Serves: 6 to 8

Ingredients:

-¾ Cup of Sugar, White

-1, 10 Ounce Package of Tofu

-1, 16 Ounce Can of Pumpkin, Puree

-½ tsp. of Salt

-1, 9 inch Pie Crust, Unbaked

-1 tsp. of Cinnamon, Ground

-¼ tsp. of Cloves, Ground

-½ tsp. of Ginger, Ground

Directions:

1. Preheat your oven to 450 degrees.

2. While your oven heats up combine your pumpkin, cinnamon, tofu, ginger, salt and sugar together in a blender. Blend completely until the mixture reaches a smooth texture and make sure to pour into your piecrust.

3. Place your piecrust into your oven and bake for 15 minutes. Reduce your oven heat to 350 degrees and bake for an additional 40 minutes. Remove from oven and allow to cool completely before serving.

Vegan Style Brownies

I do not know who is not a fan of brownies. This recipe is not only Vegan friendly, but it is also great for those who suffer from dairy and egg allergies.

Total Prep Time: 50 Minutes

Serves: 6 to 8

Ingredients:

-1 tsp. of Salt

-2 Cups of Flour, All Purpose

-1 tsp. of Baking Powder

-1 Cup of Vegetable Oil

-2 Cups of Sugar, White

-1 Cup of Water

-3/4 Cup of Cocoa Powder, Unsweetened

-1 tsp. of Vanilla Extract

Directions:

1. Preheat your oven to 350 degrees.

2. While your oven heats up use a large size mixing bowl and combine your cocoa powder, salt, flour, baking powder and sugar until all of the ingredients are mixed together. Pour this into your wet ingredients and stir until thoroughly combined.

3. Pour this into a baking pan and place into your oven to bake for the next 25 to 30 minutes or until the top of the brownies are no longer shiny. Remove from heat and allow brownies to cool for about 10 minutes before serving them.

Strawberries Mixed With Balsamic Vinegar

When you mix strawberries with some balsamic vinegar, you will help bring out the strawberries true flavor. Feel free to serve this dish with some pound cake or with some ice cream.

Total Prep Time: 1 Hour and 10 Minutes

Serves: 6

Ingredients:

-16 Ounces of Strawberries, Fresh and Cut In Half

-2 Tbsp. of Vinegar, Balsamic

-¼ tsp of Black Pepper For Taste

-¼ Cup of Sugar, White

Directions:

1. Place your strawberries into a bowl and drizzle some over the vinegar over it. Sprinkle with some sugar and stir as gently as you can to combine.

2. Grind some fresh pepper over it before serving.

Vegan Style Chocolate Pudding

This is one of the simplest recipes for dairy free chocolate pudding that you will ever find. You can use either ground cocoa or some ground chocolate to really bring out the flavor of this dessert dish.

Total Prep Time: 45 Minutes

Serves: 2

Ingredients:

-3 Tbsp. of Cornstarch

-1 ½ Cups of Milk, Soy

-¼ Cup of Sugar, White

-¼ Cup of Cocoa Powder, Unsweetened

-2 Tbsp. of Water

-¼ tsp. of Vanilla Extract

Directions:

1. In a small mixing bowl combine your water and cornstarch together until it begins to form a paste.

2. In a large sized saucepan over some medium heat combine your soymilk, cornstarch mix, sugar, ground cocoa and vanilla by stir them together. Cook and stir constantly until your pudding mixture begins to boil.

3. Remove from heat and allow the pudding to

cool completely before placing it in your fridge to chill before serving.

Delicious Vegan Style Chocolate Cake

This is one of the simplest cakes that you can make. While it is very easy to make it is also surprisingly very tasty as well.

Total Prep Time: 60 Minutes

Serves: 4

Ingredients:

-1/3 Cup of Vegetable Oil

-1 ½ Cups of Flour, All Purpose

-¼ Cup of Cocoa Powder

-1 Cup of Sugar, White

-½ tsp. of Salt

-1 Cup of Water, Warm

-1 tsp. of Vanilla Extract

-1 tsp. of Baking Soda

-1 tsp. of White Vinegar, Distilled

Directions:

1. Preheat your oven to 350 degrees. While your oven heats up grease a cake pan of your choice lightly with a generous amount of cooking spray.

2. In a medium sized mixing bowl combine your salt, flour, cocoa powder, sugar and baking soda. Add in the rest of your ingredients are stir thoroughly until the entire mixture is smooth.

3. Pour your cake batter into your cake pan and place into your oven. Bake your cake for 45 minutes. Remove from oven and allow to cool before serving.

Banana Flavored Cookies

Not only are these cookies incredibly nutritious, but they are extremely delicious as well.

Total Prep Time: 1 Hour and 10 Minutes

Serves: 8 to 10

Ingredients:

-3 Bananas, Ripe and Mashed

-1 Cup of Dates, Fresh, Pitted and Chopped Finely

-1 tsp. of Vanilla Extract

-2 Cups of Oats, Rolled

-1/3 Cup of Vegetable Oil

Directions:

1. Preheat your oven to 350 degrees.

2. While your oven heats up use a large mixing bowl to mash your bananas. Then stir in your dates, vanilla extract, oats and oil. Mix well until all of the ingredients are thoroughly mixed and allow to sit for the next 15 minutes.

3. Drop a few spoonfuls of your batter onto a greased cookie sheet and place into your oven to bake for 20 minutes or until they cookies are golden brown in color. Remove from oven and allow to cool slightly before enjoying.

Basic Vanilla Cake

This dish is somewhat spongy and dense, making it a fairly simple cake recipe to make. Feel free to top if off with your favorite kind of vegan frosting.

Total Prep Time: 50 Minutes

Serves: 6 to 8

Ingredients:

-1 Cup of Soymilk, Plain

-1 tsp. of Baking Soda

-1 Tbsp. of Vinegar, Apple Cider

-1 Cup of Sugar, White

-1 tsp. of Baking Powder

-1 ½ Cups of Flour, All Purpose and Unbleached

-1 tsp. of Baking Soda

-¼ Cup of Water

-½ tsp. of Salt

-¼ tsp. of Extract, Almond

-1/3 Cup of Canola Oil

-1 Tbsp. of Vanilla Extract

-1 Tbsp. of Lemon Juice, Fresh

Directions:

1. Preheat your oven to 350 degrees. While your oven heats up grease up a small to medium sized cake pan.

2. In a small to medium sized mixing bowl stir all of your ingredients together until you come up with a batter that is smooth and free of any lumps. Then pour your batter into your greased cake pan and place into your oven.

3. Bake your cake for 35 to 40 minutes and then remove from oven. Allow to cool slightly before removing it from the cake pan or adding some frosting to it.

Conclusion

In this book you have learned about the nutritional value of a vegan diet as well as the many benefits that it can hold you're your mind, body and soul. You have also learned about the many repercussions that come with consuming an all meat diet that can be very harmful to your overall health.

When it comes to dieting, eating the food that you love does not only mean to fill your belly until you are full or to satisfy whatever cravings that you have. Consuming food should serve as a means to nourish your body with the best substances possible as well as look at how food will affect your body and mind together as a whole.

It is important that you remember that the food you eat can affect you on many different levels that you weren't previously aware of before.

But by taking the step in the right direction towards following a vegan diet will not only leave you feeling healthier, but will help you live the longer and happier life that you deserve as a totally awesome Vegan.

If you loved what you have read in this book, please do not hesitate to leave us a review on Amazon.

If you are interested in learning more in depth information about what it means to be Vegan and how it can benefit you, check out my bestselling book on www.thethoughtflame.com. In that book you will learn about the three key benefits of becoming Vegan and read some interesting information from doctors and scientists that have studied the effects of a vegan diet on the human body.

About Us

The Thought Flame is committed to add value to its customers through various books, online courses and other resources. You can learn more about us and our books at www.thethoughtflame.com.

Don't forget to check out our amazing **online video courses** at www.thethoughtflame.com/courses/ to take your knowledge to another level.

To check out our **extraordinary collection of diet/cookbooks**, visit http://www.thethoughtflame.com/category/non-fictional/cookbooks/ .

As a part of our valued relationship with our customers, we keep providing you free promotional books, courses and other stuff on subscribing with us on our site. We have a strict anti-spam policy and assure you no spam mails will be sent to your mailbox.

To subscribe with us, visit www.thethoughtflame.com.

Like our work and would like to say thanks? Buy us a cup of coffee at www.thethoughtflame.com/coffee/

Author

Amarpreet Singh is an avid learner and his passion for education has made him travel, work and study all across the world. He holds three masters degrees, including MBA, from top universities in Asia.

He is author of dozens of books, many of which are Amazon's bestseller, varying in various topics and categories. He also teaches many online courses having thousands of students across the world.

He has a keen interest in international affairs, economics, global poverty and politics, financial markets and entrepreneurship, and strives to be part of a community that shares the same passion.

He has worked as consultant with organizations like Airbus and The World Bank. He loves travelling and learning about new cultures, and has been fortunate to live/work/travel/study in countries like India, China, Korea, US, South Africa, Japan, Philippines, Singapore, Canada etc., and learn about the culture and lifestyle in each of them. To check out more of his work, visit www.thethoughtflame.com

Printed in Great Britain
by Amazon.co.uk, Ltd.,
Marston Gate.